Contents

D1584638

Getting started...

Your checklist for a happy healthy goldfish

[ ] Fish tank/ aquarium
[ ] Background
[ ] Filter
[ ] Air pump, air tubing & air stone (optional)
[ ] Filter maturation product
[ ] Lighting
[ ] Timer
[ ] Water conditioner

[ ] Bucket (for water changes)
[ ] Flexible tubing for siphoning (or gravel cleaner)
[ ] Net
[ ] Water testing equipment
[ ] Ornamentation
[ ] Fish food

Useful books
[✓] Good Pet Guide: The Goldfish
[ ] Pet Friendly: Goldfish

Introduction

1. Goldfish

The popularity of the goldfish is no surprise. Their beautiful coloring and calm nature make them an attractive choice for a pet.

After an initial cost for setting up an aquarium, goldfish are relatively inexpensive fish to look after, with many different varieties to choose from to suit every owner.

Goldfish are hardy creatures and one of the easiest aquarium fish to care for. They are the perfect choice for people who find themselves unable to take care of a more demanding pet.

Goldfish are majestic, varied and beautiful, and as a result their aquariums can be both entertaining and calming to watch.

"I can live to be as old as 43 years."

2. Origins & habitat

Goldfish *(Carassius Auratus)* were kept as pets by fish farmers over 1000 years ago in China.

A member of the carp *(Cyprinid)* family *(which includes the colorful Koi carp)* from the east of Asia, it was first fish domesticated in China and was subsequently introduced to Europe in the late 17th century.

A wild species of Crucian carp was the first to be captured and farm-bred for eating in China, and it is the natural mutations of this breed that has brought the golden variety into existence.

These golden fish were then bred into ornamental forms as pet fish and are now classified as *'Carassius auratus var auratus'.* To this day, the best examples of exotic goldfishes in the world are imported from China.

Europe

India

CHINA

Top tips

Buyers checklist

Tank - Horizontal, big enough to support amount of fish desired.

Filter - Effective and efficient for your setup.

Gravel (substrate)

Siphon

Bucket

Fish net

Dechlorinator - Optional if dechlorinating water by other means.

Water conditioner - Before adding fish.

Fish food - Two different types, flake and pellet.

Decorations - Not too many. One should provide a shelter/ hiding spot for your fish.

Air pump - Optional if using a filter which moves the water surface sufficiently to aerate the water.

3. Life span

In the right conditions your goldfish can live up to 25 years or more! 43 years is the oldest recorded!

In a large pond, a healthy goldfish can live between 15 and 20 years and in a typical aquarium, you can expect your fish to live from 5 to 10 years.

Fishy facts

Longest goldfish

18 inches (45 cm)

Oldest goldfish

43 yrs (1956- 99)

2.

1.

Varieties

4. Colors

All goldfish have *chromatophores*, which are pigment-containing and light reflecting cells. These are what give the goldfish its color. But contrary to the name, not all goldfish are gold. Many colors are available from yellows through to black.

Black, brown and the wild green goldfish are created with different combinations of the black and yellow pigment cells, whereas blue goldfish can occur when there are no yellow pigment cells. Red or orange goldfish can come about when there are few or no black chromatophores present within the fish.

An Albino goldfish *(white)* lacks both pigments everywhere and thus will have pink eyes.

Although strange, it is not uncommon to have goldfish change color. It does happen! Black moors are known to turn vibrant orange. Whereas, black and white goldfish sometimes change colors as well in later life.

Goldfish do need a certain amount of light to maintain their color. Its much like our ability to tan. Without light they can start to lose their color and if kept in the dark too long they could turn almost white. They need between 4-8 hours of light a day. However, be careful to keep them out of direct sunlight *(it will over heat the tank and will promote the growth of algae)*, instead use fluorescent light rather than incandescent light because they give off less heat and are more energy efficient.

1. Common goldfish
2. Comet

Goldfish types

5. Common

As the name suggests, this is the most common goldfish. It is hardy, easily tamed and simple to look after. Apart from its color it is still identical to its ancient carp ancestors. Most other types of fancy goldfish have descended from this humble breed which can grow to 12 inches (30 cm). Normally orange in color, they can also be found in red and white, brownish green, or green.

6. Comet

These are an American development. They are a lot like the common goldfish but with longer deeply forked tails and slimmer bodies.

7. Shubunkin

The shubunkin has the same body shape as the comet but its coloration will be different. It will be white in color and covered in a pattern of either blue, red, brown, white or black.

8. Ryukin

The ryukin is distinguishable by it's pointy head and humped back. They have a double tail and their dorsal fins will be about twice the length of their body. They store fat in their humps and head growths if they are fed the correct high protein foods. They are fine aquarium fish that can reach up to 8.2 inches (21 cm) in length.

9. Fantail

This is the western version of the ryukin. They are usually a shorter fish with an egg shaped body. They don't have a shoulder hump but do possess a double tail fin. It's fins are oversized in proportion to its body.

10. Black Moor

These are double-tailed fish with rounded bodies and protruding eyes. A beautiful but sensitive variation that needs special attention because of its vulnerable eyes and delicate fins. Referred to as a velvet fish, they can suffer from a cotton bag like fungus if their water is not maintained *(see p22 for treatment)*.

(see p22 for treatment)

Top tips

Other breeds

Lionhead
Double-tailed fish with no dorsal fin. Short and rectangular in shape.

Ranchu
Highly regarded in Japan. No dorsal fins but do have a full face growth. More circular in shape. Sometimes referred to as the 'king of goldfish'.

Celestial
Double-tailed. Eyes that point upwards. It is a small variety and has no dorsal fin.

Pearl Scale
Round with a bulging middle. Scales, as the name suggests, appear as if there is a pearl beneath them. Should be kept in a tank of their own.

Bubble Eyed
These bubbles can be *"boxer glove"* or spherical shaped and are attached to the sides of the head. The eyes appear to be floating on the bubble itself.

They rarely have dorsal fins and are prone to eye injury.

Choosing your goldfish

11. Male or female?

Outside the breeding season it is almost impossible to tell the difference between a male and female goldfish.

During the spring the females will show signs of a plumper belly, indicating that she is full of eggs.

Males may have white *'pimples'* on their head and gills called *'tubercles'.* The little dots occur in the spring when it's mating season then disappear following fertilization *(this should not be confused with the disease 'white spot' p23).*

There are other ways to sex a goldfish, but unless you are an expert it is difficult to use these methods to great success. If you have any problems consult a member of staff in your pet shop. They should be able to help distinguish the sex of a goldfish for you.

12. Basic fish anatomy

A quick guide to the different parts of the anatomy of your goldfish *(see opposite for things to look out for when initially choosing your goldfish).*

Top tips

Moving

When you move your fish into a new aquarium or clean the tank make sure that:

➔ You don't shock your fish from with the change in temperature and light.

➔ You float the bag or container that is holding your fish in the new water for about half an hour so they get used to the change in temperature gradually.

Set up a tank a week before you buy your first fish.

✔

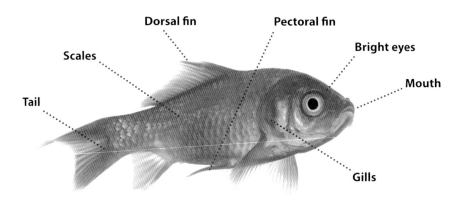

Dorsal fin

Pectoral fin

Scales

Bright eyes

Mouth

Tail

Gills

13. Know your goldfish

Here are a few things to keep an eye on to ensure that the goldfish you are choosing is fit and healthy.

→ Scales
Ensure your goldfish is free from sore looking areas or woolly looking fungal growths.

→ Eyes
Should be bright and clear, never opaque as this can be a symptom of a sick fish.

→ Breathing
If the gills of the fish are moving very rapidly this can be symptomatic of a lack of oxygen in the tank or a breathing problem.

→ Fins
Should be erect and not damaged *(see health section p22-23).*

→ Color
The color of the fish should be dense and vibrant.

→ Movement
The goldfish should seem alert. Your fish should be swimming effortlessly. Long-finned goldfish will swim more slowly.

→ Appetite
A healthy fish will have a healthy appetite. Be wary of a fish with too big an appetite.

→ Mucus
Your fish should have a clear layer of mucus all over its body to help protect it from infection.

Housing your goldfish

14. Fishbowls

If you can, avoid goldfish bowls altogether. They're too small and often difficult to maintain properly.

A bowl will stunt the growth of your fish and this will cause many other health problems as a result. If you have to keep your fish in a bowl, do so only for a short period of time *(as a bowl is unfiltered and will quickly become toxic)* and only fill the bowl halfway. The bowl will be wider around the middle and will have a greater surface area which will allow more oxygen to get to your fish.

Watch out for rapid movements of the gills, as this can be an indication that the goldfish isn't getting enough oxygen and requires a tank. When you can afford to buy a tank do so! It's not that expensive and your fish will be far happier!

15. Tanks

Tank size is an important step to becoming a responsible goldfish owner.

Remember that in a small tank, water can deteriorate rapidly, while a tank that is too large can be awkward for a beginner. You should as a rule have *2.2 gallons* (10 liters) of water per goldfish. Choose a tank that has more water surface than depth if possible. A large surface area will provide more oxygen for your fish. Rectangular ones are better for goldfish, as they tend to need more room than other types of fish.

Tank should contain: *A filter, plants, rocks and ornaments to make it interesting and provide a hiding place for your fish (see p10-11).*

(see p10-11).

Top tips

Cleaning
You need to clean your goldfish tank regularly. Make sure that you:

→ Replace part of the water every 1 or 2 weeks.

→ Change 20-30% of the water each time, never all of it at once.

→ Clean ornaments and gravel.

→ Let new water stand for a couple of days so that the chlorine evaporates or use dechlorinating liquid before putting it into your tank.

→ Don't overfeed your fish as uneaten food can make the water dirty.

16. **Things to remember**

There are a few things to remember when finding a suitable place for your tank, all of which are best planned ahead of time:

→ **Sunlight**

Pick an area of the room that gets indirect sunlight. Direct sunlight won't benefit your tank. It will promote the growth of algae which should be avoided as the light can change the temperature of your tank and in turn shock your fish.

→ **Temperature**

Fish are sensitive to drafts and temperature changes. You should place the tank where drafts don't exist. If you pick an area too close to a window or door, it can result in cold air getting to the tank. You should pick a part of the room where the temperature is as constant as possible.

→ **Power**

Your tank will need to be near its own safe power point for easy access to electricity.

→ **Equipment**

Think about where you will place your pump, filters and supplies in relation to the tank (see p16- 17 for more information of filters).

→ **Support**

Fish tanks when full with water, filters and accessories are extremely heavy. Ensure you have a suitable place to support it. A smaller tank can be supported on a very solid piece of furniture, whereas lightweight furniture will almost certainly break under the weight of the water.

→ **Cushioning**

A cork or polystyrene sheet can be placed beneath your tank to absorb any irregularities in the surface. It is vital that any base is level for your tank.

→ **Space**

Inevitably you will need to change water as well as position things in the interior of your tank. Make sure that your tank is positioned in an easily accessible location. You should also set aside an area near to the tank so that you can store all the tank supplies within easy reach.

→ **Water**

Even if your fish are kept correctly in a reasonably sized aquarium with filtration, it will still require regular water changes. In a normal sized tank, a water change of about 20-30% is still required on a weekly basis. This is needed to help remove all the waste as well as providing nutrient-enriched water.

Setting up

17. Getting up and running

Once you've chosen the right spot for your tank you can start setting it up.

Substrate

We recommend gravel with a diameter of 3-6 mm to cover the bottom of the tank. Before adding the gravel rinse with clean water. Put a 1 cm (1/3 inch) layer of gravel in the bottom of the tank.

Bucket

The tank can now be half-filled with faucet water at room temperature. It is best to put a dish on the gravel and pour water first on the dish, letting the water overflow, thus not disturbing the substrate.

Equipment

Attach the filter to the inside of the tank. It will remove suspended matter from the water as well as providing an environment for beneficial bacterial that remove dissolved toxins.

Water

Water should be treated to eradicate any toxins so your tank is an environment your goldfish can survive in happily *(see p14)*.

Aquatic plants

You can choose natural or artificial aquatic plants. Natural plants are decorative and add to the biological equilibrium of the tank. Artificial plants are purely aesthetic but easier to maintain *(see p20)*. Don't overcrowd your tank with plants.

Decoration

You can also decorate with stones or roots. You can get these from your pet store. Make sure that your fish have space to swim around and that decorations are secured. Sterilize decorations in boiling water before use *(be careful to select stones that do not alter your tanks water chemistry)*.

Mat

Place a sheet of cork, polystyrene or a specialized tank mat *(from your pet store)* underneath your tank. This will make sure that all imperfections on the support surface do not effect the glass of your tank.

The tank

Create a decorative and imaginative place for your fish to live using rocks, shells and various objects that will not harm your fish.

Ideal temperature
Keep your aquarium between
21 - 24 Degrees C
or
70 - 75 Degrees F

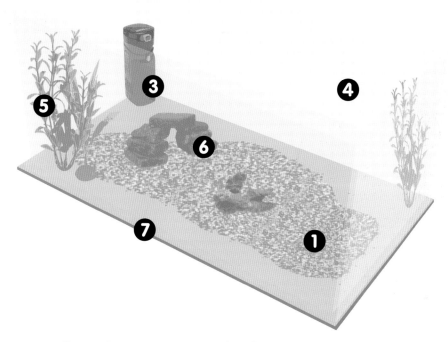

18. Releasing your goldfish

Before adding any newly purchased fish, you'll need to make sure the tank has reached a biological balance. If you don't do this, you could experience problems with your tank and your fishes health!

You'll need to test the most important water levels. General hardness, nitrite, ammonia nitrate, carbonate hardness and pH level. This can be done easily with the right testing kit. If after cycling *(see p14-15)* or the addition of beneficial bacterial, the levels are right then you begin adding your fish *(see p21)*.

Goldfish food guide

19. Feeding

Goldfish are omnivores and as such eat both animal and vegetable matter.

An important thing to know about goldfish is that they are *'continual feeders',* which essentially means that goldfish are always on the look out for food. They will spend most of their days hunting around for their next meal. Goldfish should be fed small but frequent meals.

If a goldfish eats too much dry food at one time, it can develop gas or constipation problems that can be very severe. Soaking the dry food before feeding can help prevent some of these problems.

1.

20. Five minute rule

It's hard to determine the right amount of food to feed your goldfish. This is a skill you can only gain after experience. A good rule to follow is to only feed your fish what they can eat in 5 minutes.

Goldfish will eat whatever amount of food is given to them, they don't ever seem to get full. This may seem humorous, but do not fall into the trap of overfeeding your goldfish as their own greed can prove fatal. They can eat so much that they will suffer serious health problems as their stomach is about the same size as their eye.

Be responsible with your feeding routine, maintain the water quality and your goldfish will thrive.

2.

Overfeeding

If you over feed your Goldfish, food being pushed in mouth literally pushes food out the back end. When overfed this will occur before food had a chance to be fully digested. If your goldfish feces look just like his food, this could be an indication of overfeeding.

3.

21. How often?

Goldfish should be fed 2/3 times a day but ensure that it is a small amount.

If you happen to miss a feeding time for your fish, don't make up for it in the next feeding session by doubling the food portion.

In smaller tanks it is also better to feed a pellet food as this produces less waste. Less waste means better water quality.

22. Choice

Give your goldfish some variety in their diet. Pellet and flake foods are available, but you may also like to try feeding them other foods such as peas every now and again as this offers a nice change. However, only feed peas rarely, as they can cause swim bladder problems if given too often.

If you are going away on holiday, you can purchase a *'goldfish feeder block'* from your pet shop. This is a specially designed block which dissolves slowly over a predetermined time by releasing food trapped within it *(you can get 3 day, 7 day and 14 day blocks)*. If you are going on holiday for longer, get a friend or neighbor who you can rely on to feed your goldfish. Give them instructions on the amount of food to give them, as people easily feel sorry for your fish and overfeed them.

Healthy goldfish can easily stand a day or two without food.

1. Goldfish pellets
2. Goldfish flake food
3. 14 day feeder block

Water quality

23. Water chemistry

Before you're ready to add water to your tank, you'll need to ensure that the water is suitable for your goldfish to survive. Goldfish prefer slightly hard water with neutral to moderate alkaline pH levels.

You will need to add good dechlorinator. Some water companies use chloramine as a disinfectant as well as chlorine, so try to use a product that removes chloramine and chlorine. A dechlorinator that isn't designed to remove both will break chloramine down into chlorine and ammonia. The chlorine is obviously removed by the product, but the ammonia is left in the tank, poisoning your goldfish.

24. Cycling

When you are setting up your new tank, it is important to carry out a thorough *'cycling'* so that beneficial bacteria can be established. You will need to do this before adding your goldfish.

The complete *'cycling'* of the tank is necessary to raise your goldfish successfully. If toxin levels get too high the fish can die, so regular testing is advised.

Firstly, you should monitor ammonia and nitrite levels *(using a water testing kit pictured opposite)*. These should ideally read 0, though 0.5 ammonia is acceptable. If levels are high, small water changes everyday of at least 10-20% will stabilize them.

This process normally takes about 7 days to complete, though it does depend on your tank size and faucet water quality to begin with. Patience is key here, if you try to rush this stage and add fish too soon or too many at once, the whole system will fail, leading to fatalities and more hard work to stabilize your water quality.

When ammonia and nitrite levels are reduced down to 0 and nitrates are all that you have left, the tank is fully cycled. The only thing to do now is carry out regular water changes *(as a rule 10-20% water change every week depending on the toxin levels)*.

You can now add your goldfish.

Beneficial bacteria

There are products on the market that can help add beneficial bacteria to your aquarium. This can help you with introducing your fish more quickly. If interested ask your pet store for details.

25. Tank monitoring

Once goldfish and plants are in the tank, you'll notice initially that ammonia levels will rise. This is due to the subsequent food waste, fish feces and plant decay being released.

Ideally you need the ammonia under 1 ppm *(parts per million)* and nitrites under 2 ppm by performing water changes. These *(and all water changes)* should be done with temperature matched, dechlorinated water. Test your water in the morning and every night. If ammonia climbs higher than 1 ppm, do a water change of 50%. These levels will usually rise day to day so closely monitoring them is vital. The ammonia will disappear first, then 1-2 weeks after, nitrites will begin to disappear. It's about this time that you should start seeing nitrates appear on the kits. At around the 20-30 day mark the tank should be nearly completely cycled.

After the tank has cycled, you will just need to keep an eye on the toxin levels and do weekly water changes to keep the nitrates to a safe minimum *(40 ppm or less)*.

26. Nitrites

Nitrites are toxins that poison your goldfish and effect their ability to intake oxygen. Aquarium tonic salt will act as a barrier against these toxins and will promote healthy gill function, increasing oxygen intake, reducing stress and making life for your fish a lot easier.

There is no need to have aquarium salt in the tank constantly, although having it in the tank at very low levels can have some beneficial effects against stress and disease. You should only add salt in a higher concentration when you notice signs of disease, stress or symptoms of nitrite poisoning *(see 'Top tips')*.

Testing the water will show whether you have an increased nitrite level in your tank. In order to reduce these levels you can, as a rule, add 1 tbsp per 19 liters of water *(follow specific product instructions if different)*. When starting, you'll want to make the salinity rises gradually so as not to stress your goldfish.

It's important to remember that salt cannot be filtered out, or evaporated from the water. If you're replacing water due to loss from evaporation, make sure that no further salt is added. Once the signs of disease or stress dissipate you can return the tank gradually to its normal level.

Top tips

Nitrite poisoning symptoms

→ Fish gasp for breath at the water surface.

→ Fish hover around water outlets.

→ Fish show lack of energy.

→ Tan or brown gills.

→ Rapid gill movement.

→ Ragged looking fins.

→ Black spots.

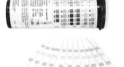

27. Water testing

Buy a test kit so that you can see the levels of ammonia, nitrites and nitrates in the water.

It vital to keep testing when your starting out as this is a crucial time.

What is a filter?

Filtration is a process involving mechanical, biological and chemical means to remove organic and chemical polluting elements that are present in an aquarium.

Filtration

28. Three kinds of water filtration

→ **Mechanical**

Mechanical filtration of water is achieved by passing the water through a screen or sponge removing pieces of debris from the water.

→ **Chemical**

Chemical filtration is achieved by passing water through carbon and/or zeolite (*zeolite is a natural occurring porous mineral that is now widely synthesized*). The carbon removes a lot of toxins from the water (*like chlorine*), zeolite helps remove ammonia.

→ **Biological**

Biological filtration of water is carried out by certain types of bacteria that live on gravel, the surface of glass, tank ornaments, plastic plants, filter sponges and bio-balls.

Filter types

29. Sponge filter

This is the most basic type of filter. It consists simply of a sponge through which water is pulled by the rising air bubbles of an air pump. Initially it will filter out impurities and debris. But once matured it will develop a type of biological filtration. Bacteria grows on the sponge and will remove additional toxins. It will however, take a little time to mature to an optimum level *(to speed things up, you can find products on the market that will add these beneficial bacteria directly into the water)*. The sponge itself is capable of supporting a very large amount of beneficial bacteria, but in an average tank they will need cleaning about once a month *(You can do this easily without harming the good bacteria by simply rinsing in water)*.

30. Internal power filter

This type of filter uses an electrical powered centrifugal pump to pull water through the filter material *(sponge or other material)*. They can create a more powerful circulation than their air-powered counterparts. This filter is best suited to aquariums in the 2-4 ft range, and is also useful when used along with external canister filters for larger aquariums.

31. External canister filter

This works on the same principle as internal power filters. As the name suggests, they operate from outside of the tank and pull water into the filter through an inlet tube. Water is then returned into the tank via another tube, which can be fitted with a spray bar to increase aeration *(increase oxygen)*. They are a great choice for larger tanks containing plants.

Undergravel filters (UGF)

These look tidier than other filter alternatives and have a large surface area for filtration. The downside being that they can take up to 6 month to mature.

They work by sucking water from the tank down through the gravel, which acts as a mechanical and biological filtration media.

The water is drawn through the undergravel filter plates and into uplift tubes by an airpump or powerhead. ✓

Black moor

Tank care

Always remember!
Cleaning the fish tank is essential. *"The solution to pollution is dilution".*

32. A clean tank is a happy tank

Regular water changes are vital to keep your goldfish happy and healthy.

All too often, the water is left until it gets so dirty that the goldfish can no longer be seen. Then it's given a complete clear-out, with everything scrubbed clean and the water changed completely. This kind of leap from one extreme to the other should be avoided as not only is it traumatic for the fish, but the new water, if left untreated, will give them *'chemical shock'*. Your tank should have regular water changes of around 20-30% with dechlorinated, temperature matched water.

33. Digestion

Goldfish digest food in much the same way we do, and just like us they excrete the waste, both solids and liquid. Their fluid excretion is the equivalent to our urine.

Fish perform a process called *'osmosis'*. This is the drawing in of the water through the skin. The fish then excrete their 'urine' *(full of ammonia)* back out through the skin and into the water. Ammonia irritates the gills and causes a protective mucus to form. This reduces the intake of oxygen and so the fish can be seen gasping for breath at the surface trying to get extra air, even if the tank water may look perfectly clean and clear. The ammonia produced by the fish is usually acted upon in mature water by *'beneficial bacteria'*, which convert it to another compound called nitrite. This is equally poisonous and also invisible. These levels can be brought back down to normal levels with the use of filters, water changes and the addition of beneficial bacteria to the tank *(see p14 - 15 for information on tank cycling and water testing)*.

34. Recommended items

A few items that will ensure that keeping goldfish is a simple and enjoyable experience for both you and your goldfish.

→ → Siphon

Used for making water changes and removing wastes from the gravel.

→ → Air pump

The air pump is used to pump air through a small tube which is connected to a filter. An air pump is used in a biological filter to aerate the surface where bacteria grows and to displace water *(increasing oxygen in the water)*.

→ → Net

Use a net to catch fish when moving them from tank to tank. Make sure you have a suitable net for all your fish *(big enough for your biggest)*.

→ → Roots/ wood

Roots/ wood can provide a few places for your goldfish to hide, making it a more interesting place to live and to look at. Be sure to only get wood from your pet shop as driftwood will need specialist cleaning before it is safe to go in your tank.

→ → Algae scrubber

Once your tank is matured, algae is likely to start growing. Algae is removed easily from the inside glass with an algae scrubber *(pictured)*. Too much light stimulates algae growth. If algae starts taking over, move your aquarium out of the sun.

Top tips

Tank decorating

Decorating your tank is a personal thing and you will obviously do this to your own specifications, but here are a few things to keep in mind:

→ Gravel, decorative ornaments, artificial and live plants can help to create a exciting home for your fish.

→ Avoid sharp objects in the tank. You could end up with an injured fish. This is especially true with fancy species with large fins or bubble eyes.

→ Choose plants of varying sizes to create a more natural look in the tank. This will allow the fish a refuge from the bright light when the tank lights first come on.

→ Artificial plants are often a better idea with your goldfish, as they tend to dig up, as well as feed on the living plants.

Plants

Make sure you select plants suitable for cold water aquariums as most types of plants are tropical.

35. Natural or artificial

You can choose natural or artificial aquatic plants. Natural plants are very decorative as well as being important to the biological equilibrium of the tank. They'll reduce water contamination and, in the day, they will produce oxygen which is essential to the fish.

Artificial plants do not contribute to the oxygen content in the tank but they do add places for your goldfish to seek shelter and they ensure that you aquarium is an interesting place to live in and watch.

36. Growing plants

See opposite 'Top tips' for types of aquarium plants.

If you are looking to maintain live aquatic plants then you may find that the usual one or two lamp setups usually sold with tanks are not sufficient. Consider adding one more lamp.

It is important to remember not to keep the lights on more than 11 hours a day as the overuse of light will encourage algae growth. Keep direct sunlight off the tank as it too will rapidly stimulate growth of algae and could cause temperature changes that will stress your goldfish.

Fertilize lightly with trace elements but stay away from any that contain phosphates. Phosphates will give algae an unwanted boost. Your goldfish will provide a perfect amount of *'macro'* nutrients in their waste in order for the survival of your plants. All you will need to supply are the *'micro'* nutrients.

Adding your fish

37. Acclimatizing your fish

Your fish will come in a plastic bag.

Inside this bag is the water from your pet shop. This will contain water of the same maturity and temperature as the pet shop aquarium it came from. Your own fish tank conditions will come as a shock to your new fish and therefore, you shouldn't just drop him into the tank. You will need to 'acclimatize' the goldfish first.

With your new fish held within the bag, float it in your tank water. This will help bring the temperature of the water in the bag to around the same as the tank.

After 10 minutes, add a cup of water from your tank into the bag and let the bag float another 5 minutes.

After the 5 minutes add a further 2 cups water, let the bag float for another 10 minutes.

Finally, carefully release your fish from the bag using a net. Try not to let the bag water fall into the tank.

Myth: 3 second memory?
Goldfish are more intelligent than first thought. They can remember the person who feeds them regularly and they can also be taught to follow a routine.

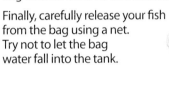

Top tips

Plants

Anubias 'Living plastic plant'. Very hardy and slow growing. Give it bright light for faster growth.

Crinum thaianum 'Onion plant' Looks like a leek.

Echinodorus 'Sword plant' Likes soil in root area. Place in shallow pots.

Elodea 'Anacharis'. Floated/ planted into gravel.

Hygrophila difformis 'Water wisteria'. Often confused with Ceratopteris thalictroides.

Nymphoides aquatica 'Banana plant'. Push "bananas" halfway into gravel. Goldfish eat the tender new shoots.

Ceratophyllum submersum 'Hornwort'. A floating plant with no roots.

Java Fern. Long, dark and light green leaves. In cold water its leaves will grow up to 10 cm (4 inches). Strong root system that helps them attach to rocks.

Cryptocoryne petchii A member of the 'arum' family. Well developed roots. Can grow up to 15 cm (6 inches) leaves. Likes a lot of light so plant in the front of the tank.

Health

38. Prevention

Fish are easily stressed in poor water conditions, which can lower their immune system, in turn leaving them open to all kinds of diseases. The best way to keep your water quality high is to do partial water changes and test the water weekly.

Glass tapping!
Tapping on the glass can cause stress to your goldfish, and at worst damage their internal swim bladder which helps them balance.

39. Goldfish diseases

a. Large external parasites

Condition: Most common are fish lice and anchor worms. Lice appear as round discs *(or bugs)* attached to the fish. Anchor worms look like thin bits of white/ green thread hanging from the fish.
Treatment: Choose an anti-external parasite treatment *(once the parasite has left the fish follow instructions carefully to see if you can use aquarium tonic salt alongside it)*. It's advisable to move your sick goldfish to a quarantine tank during treatment.

b. Fungus

Condition: A bacterial infection that looks like white furry patches on your fish.
Treatment: Easily treated with an anti-fungus treatment. Aquarium tonic salt is also useful during treatment, although check instructions before using them together.

c. Slime disease

Condition: Excess mucus covering the body making the fish a cloudy grey.
Treatment: Choose a slime disease treatment.

d. Dropsy

Condition: Scales stick out from the fishes body. This is a bacterial infection. In this case your fish has a very slim chance of surviving. Condition may be preceded by eyes bulging out of the socket *(a condition called Pop eye)*.
Treatment: Choose an anti-bacterial treatment.

e. Fin/tail/mouth rot

Condition: This disease can be contracted when the fins are damaged in some way. Starting off as a white edge on the fins, progressing onto tearing apart of the fins. Your goldfish will often be lethargic and eyes will have a white sheen to them.
Treatment: Choose an anti-fin rot treatment *(follow instructions carefully to see if you can use aquarium tonic salt alongside it)*. Your goldfish will probably grow back damaged areas, although this will take some time.

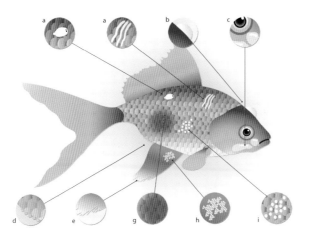

Gasping fish

If your fish seem to be gasping at the surface for air, shaking, rubbing against things, hiding or swimming strangely take these steps to treat them and hopefully reduce any disease symptoms.

Clean the fish tank and change about 20-40% of the water.

Vacuum the gravel and remove built up dirt in it. ✓

f. Swim bladder problems

Condition: The swim bladder is a gas filled sack inside fish that helps it to balance. Problems with it can affect your fishes ability to swim properly.
Treatment: Swim bladder control treatments or an anti-internal bacterial treatment *(follow instructions to see if you can use aquarium tonic salt* alongside it).*

g. Ulcers

Condition: Red sore or sores on the side of the fish.
Treatment: These need quick treatment as they can worsen quickly. They can sometimes lead to a second fungal infection. Choose an anti-ulcer treatment or anti-bacterial treatment *(follow instructions carefully to see if you can use aquarium tonic salt* too).*

h. Velvet disease

Condition: Fish will look much like it's been dusted with icing sugar and covered in tiny white spots. These will be far smaller than those associated to 'White spot'. Fish often rub against rocks or ornaments to try and remove the spots.
Treatment: Anti-velvet disease treatment *(follow instructions carefully to see if you can use aquarium tonic salt* alongside it).*

i. White spot

Condition: Small spots all over the fish. Usually first seen on the fins. The spots are the egg sacks of a parasite. Fish will rub against rocks to try and remove the spots.
Treatment: Get an off the shelf anti-white spot treatment.

* What is aquarium tonic salt?

Aquarium tonic salt has been proven to reduce toxicity levels in the aquarium.

The salt boosts the amount of ions in the water which give the fish protection against nitrites.

The tonic salt can kill parasites and is a method of curing fungus infections on fish.

Titles in series

the **kitten**
Top tips for a happy healthy pet

the **goldfish**
Top tips for a happy healthy pet

the **rabbit**
Top tips for a happy healthy pet

the **hamster**
Top tips for a happy healthy pet

the **gerbil**
Top tips for a happy healthy pet

the **dwarf rabbit**
Top tips for a happy healthy pet

the **puppy**
Top tips for a happy healthy pet

the **guinea pig**
Top tips for a happy healthy pet

the **dwarf hamster**
Top tips for a happy healthy pet

the **degu**

Copyright © 2017 Magnet & Steel Ltd
Publisher: Magnet & Steel Ltd
Printed and bound in South Korea.

Magnet & Steel Ltd
Unit 6
Vale Business Park,
Llandow, United Kingdom. CF71 7PF
sales@magnetsteel.com
www.magnetsteel.com

ALL RIGHTS RESERVED
No parts of this book may be reproduced or transmitted in any form or by any means, electronic or mechanical, including photocopying, recording, or by any information storage and retrieval system, without permission in writing from the Publisher.

The advice contained in this book is provided as general information only. It does not relate to any specific case and should not be substituted for the advice or guidance of a licensed veterinary practitioner. Magnet & Steel Publishing Ltd do not accept liability or responsibility for any consequences resulting from the use of or reliance upon the information contained herein. No animal was harmed in the making of this book.